BACK-TO-SCHOOL
Mini-Plays for Beginning Readers

20 Reproducible Plays About Following Routines, Cooperating, Making New Friends, and More!

NEW YORK • TORONTO • LONDON • AUCKLAND • SYDNEY

MEXICO CITY • NEW DELHI • HONG KONG • BUENOS AIRES

Teaching *Resources*

The following activities and plays have been adapted from their original sources and
used by permission of the authors.

"All About Me" Banner, "We're in _____ !" Banner, and "Hurry Up!" by Deborah Schecter.

"All About Us" by Kathleen M. Hollenbeck.

"First Day of School" by Betsy Franco.

"Fish School," "How We Go to School," and "New in School" by Carol Pugliano-Martin.

"Lunch Crunch" by Liza Charlesworth.

"Many Ways to Say 'Hello'" by Joan Novelli.

"Show and Tell" and "Mary Went to the Library" by Sheryl Ann Crawford and Nancy I. Sanders.

All other plays by Dorothy Jean Sklar.

Cover design by Brian LaRossa
Cover illustrations by Peggy Tagel
Interior design by Solas
Interior illustrations by Maxie Chambliss, Sue Dennen, Shelley Dieterichs, Mark Hicks, Rusty Fletcher,
Anne Kennedy, Ellen Joy Sasaki, and Bari Weissman

ISBN-13: 978-0-545-05064-7
ISBN-10: 0-545-05064-2

Contents

Introduction

Get the school year off to a smooth start with these short, super-easy plays that tap into the emotions and excitement stirred up by those first days and weeks. You can use the plays as springboards for establishing rules and routines, encouraging positive behavior, helping children get to know one another, and building classroom community. In addition, the plays in this collection will help children get a great start in reading as they learn to love to read!

The plays include the following features:

❖ Rhyming sentences with repetitive and predictable text that support beginning readers

❖ Repeated and recognizable high-frequency words

❖ Short, easy-to-read formats that are perfect for repeated reading—a key component in building oral fluency

❖ Multiple speaking parts that make them ideal for Readers Theater

Tips

❖ Copy the plays onto transparencies for use on an overhead projector.

❖ Before reading "A Brand-New Year," page 17, fill in your students' grade on the blank lines.

❖ On page 20 of "Many Ways to Say 'Hello,'" have children write the way they say *hello*. This might be in English, or in any other language children speak at home.

Using the Plays

You can use the plays in this collection in a variety of ways with your class. Try these tips and suggestions:

Introducing the Plays

✱ Read a play aloud and then review words that may be unfamiliar or difficult for children to read.

✱ Discuss strategies children can use to decode words they do not know, such as finding beginning or ending sounds, breaking a word into parts, and using picture clues. Provide background for any concepts or vocabulary that might be unfamiliar to children.

Building Fluency

The length of the plays as well as features such as rhyme, repetition, and predictable text make them well suited for fluency practice—so important for building reading comprehension. The plays contain a range of punctuation and phrasing, two key elements of fluency. For example, the line-by-line arrangement of very short sentences helps children identify phrase boundaries.

Read a play aloud several times while children follow along. Model how pacing, expression, punctuation and inflection help communicate meaning. For example, to demonstrate how punctuation affects expression and meaning, on chart paper, write the same sentence from a play three times, first using a period, then an exclamation point, and finally, a question mark.

> Are you new here.
>
> Are you new here!
>
> Are you new here?

(From "New in School," page 38)

Read each sentence aloud and ask children to describe how your voice changed with each reading. How does this change the meaning? Repeat the demonstration and then invite children to read aloud with you.

Choral and Echo Reading

Choral and echo reading are effective techniques for giving children the repeated practice they need to build fluency. To do choral reading, you and your students read together as a group. This encourages children to read at the same pace and with the same phrasing and intonation as the rest of the group. This approach works well with many of the plays because of their predictability and repetition. In echo reading, you read a line and children then repeat it, echoing your expression, tone, and pacing. Plays that work well for choral and echo reading include: "Hurry Up! Hurry Up!," page 13, "How We Go to School," page 15, "It's Cleanup Time," page 26, "Lunch Crunch," page 28, and "Mary Went to the Library," page 46.

Readers Theater

Readers Theater is an excellent way to build fluency. It allows all children to participate and succeed. English Language Learners, in particular, benefit from listening to the repeated readings of the text by other children. And as the group works together on fluency skills such as expression, intonation, and phrasing, group members can offer each other feedback and encouragement.

Tip

Have children use a highlighter to distinguish their speaking parts and lines.

To prepare for Readers Theater, divide the class into groups. Give a copy of the play to each child. Assign different speaking parts to children or have group members choose them together. Tell each group to read and rehearse their play many times. Give children plenty of practice time, reminding them to pay attention to the good reading behaviors they learned. Once the members of a group feel confident with their reading invite them to perform the play for the rest of the class. Plays with distinct characters, such as "Lost and Found," page 22, "Fish School," page 24, "A Pie for Pigs," page 30, "New in School," page 38, and "Show and Tell," page 44 are well suited to Readers Theater. "Reading Friends," page 40, is a good play for pairs of children to work on together.

Connections to the Language Arts Standards

Mid-continent Research for Education and Learning (McREL), a nationally recognized nonprofit organization, has compiled and evaluated national and state standards—and proposed what teachers should provide for their students to grow proficient in language arts, among other curriculum areas. The plays and activities in this book support these standards for grades K–2 in the following areas:

Reading

◆ Uses basic elements of phonetic and structural analysis

◆ Understands level-appropriate sight words and vocabulary

◆ Uses self-correction strategies

◆ Uses reading skills and strategies to understand and interpret a variety of literary texts, including plays

◆ Reads aloud familiar texts with fluency and expression

◆ Relates texts to personal experiences

Listening and Speaking

◆ Recites and responds to familiar texts with patterns

◆ Uses different voice level, phrasing, and intonation for different situations

◆ Makes contributions in class and group discussions

◆ Follows rules of conversation and group discussion

Life Skills

◆ Works cooperatively within a group to complete tasks, achieve goals, and solve problems

◆ Demonstrates respect for others' rights, feelings, and points of view

◆ Takes the initiative in interacting with others

◆ Uses appropriate strategies when making requests of others

Source: Kendall, J. S., & Marzano, R. J. (2004). *Content knowledge: A compendium of standards and benchmarks for K–12 education* (4th ed.). Aurora, CO: Mid-Continent Research for Education and Learning. Online database: http://www.mcrel.org/standards-benchmarks/

Extension Activities

Use the following teacher-tested ideas and activities to further explore and extend the topics and themes of the plays—and help build classroom community at the start of the school year.

Good Things

Welcome students to a new year with goodie bags!

Place a pencil, a fun-shaped eraser, a Lifesavers candy, and a penny inside a paper lunch bag (or use the goodie bags available at party stores.) Punch a hole at the top of each bag and tie on a tag that says: "Good Things for This Year!" As children explore the contents of their bags, explain the significance of each item:

- ❖ A pencil to write down all the good ideas you'll have.
- ❖ An eraser because it's all right to make mistakes.
- ❖ A lifesaver because I'm always here for you.
- ❖ And a penny for good luck.

(Contributed by Stacey Bonds.)

We're in _____ ! Banner

Make this banner at the start of the school year to help the children in your class get to know one another and develop a sense of community.

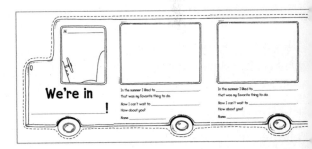

Use the pattern showing the front of the school bus (page 9) to fill in your students' grade and your name. Invite a child to draw a picture of you driving the bus! Then give each child a copy of the pattern on page 10. Let children draw a picture of themselves in the window, complete the prompt, and sign their name. To assemble the banner, begin with the front of the bus and tape to the other pattern pages. (Or use clothespins to clip the pages to a length of string strung across your classroom.

Toss and Tell

Use this activity as an icebreaker to spark a lively round of sharing among the children in your class.

Make two oversized number cubes by covering square tissue boxes with craft paper. On one cube, write the numbers 1–6. On the other, write things children can tell about themselves or their families, for example:

- ❖ my favorite stories
- ❖ my favorite foods
- ❖ things I like to do
- ❖ things my family does together
- ❖ places I've visited
- ❖ words that describe me

Literature Links

These books capture the excitement—and apprehension—that many children feel at the beginning of the school year.

Chrysanthemum by Kevin Henkes (Greenwillow, 1991)

First Day, Hooray! by Nancy Poydar (Holiday House, 1999)

First Day Jitters by Julie Danneberg (Whispering Coyote, 2000)

It's Time for School, Stinky Face by Lisa McCourt (Bridgewater Books, 2000)

The Kissing Hand by Audrey Penn (Child & Family Press, 1993)

Lunch Bunnies by Kathryn Lasky (Little, Brown, 1996)

Sumi's First Day of School Ever by Soyung Pak (Viking, 2003)

Wemberly Worried by Kevin Henkes (Greenwillow Books, 2000)

Where Are You Going, Manyoni? by Catherine Stock (Morrow, 1993)

Will I Have a Friend? by Miriam Cohen (MacMillan, 1967)

Gather children in a circle and model how to play: Toss the cubes, then tell something about yourself based on how the cubes land—for example, if you rolled a 2 and "my favorite foods," you tell two foods you like. Let children continue, taking turns tossing the cubes and sharing something about themselves.

(Contributed by Deborah Rovin-Murphy.)

All About Me Banner

This banner lets children share something that makes them special.

Give each child a copy of the pattern on page 11. Have children complete the prompt and then invite them to personalize the body outline to resemble themselves. Have yarn, ribbon, fabric scraps, wiggle eyes, glue, and other arts and crafts materials on hand for them to enhance their work. Then have children cut out their shapes and tape together so that the figures look like they are holding hands. Display the banner on a bulletin board or above your chalkboard or whiteboard.

Cafeteria Behavior Booster

Help children learn the routines and appropriate behavior for lunchtime in the cafeteria.

Plan a mid-morning snack in the cafeteria. Invite cafeteria staff to participate so that children can meet lunchtime helpers. At snack time, take children to the cafeteria (following whatever procedure they'll normally use at lunchtime.) Let them pick up trays and snacks, and then sit at a table. Take time to let children share some of the things they noticed their classmates doing well—for example, saying please and thank you to the lunch line workers and carrying their trays with two hands. Before returning to the classroom, model how to clean up the table, dispose of trash, sort any recyclables, and put trays where they belong. Then let children do the same.

(Contributed by Charlotte Sassman.)

M _____

We're in

!

In the summer I liked to _____.

that was *my favorite thing to do.*

Now I can't wait to _____.

How about you?

Name _____

All About Me

Some kids tell funny jokes.
Others are great in art.
What makes me special?
What sets me apart?

_____

_____

Name _____

First Day of School

Child 1: I'm happy!

Child 2: I'm ready!

Child 3: I'm silly!

Child 4: I'm sad!

Child 5: I'm jolly!

Child 6: I'm jumpy!

Child 7: I'm dizzy!

Child 8: I'm scared!

All: We have so many feelings
now that school is to start.
We'll miss some things at home,
but we know we'll get smart!

The End

Hurry Up! Hurry Up!

Child 1:   Get out of bed.

All: Hurry up! Hurry up!

Child 2:   Brush my teeth.

All: Hurry up! Hurry up!

Child 3:   Get dressed.

All: Hurry up! Hurry up!

Child 4:   Eat breakfast.

All: Hurry up! Hurry up!

Child 5:   Take my lunch.

All: Hurry up! Hurry up!

Child 6:   Get my bus.

All: Hurry up! Hurry up!

Child 7:   It is the first day of school.

All: Hurry up! Hurry up!

The End

How We Go to School

Sing to the tune of "Mary Had a Little Lamb"

> **Characters**
> Bus Group   Train Group
> Bicycle Group   Walking Group
> Car Group

Bus Group: We go riding on a bus,
on a bus,
on a bus.
We go riding on a bus.
That's how we get to school.

Bicycle Group: We go riding on our bikes,
on our bikes,
on our bikes.
We go riding on our bikes.
That's how we get to school.

Car Group: We go riding in a car,
in a car,
in a car.
We go riding in a car.
That's how we get to school.

........➤

Train Group: We go riding on a train,
on a train,
on a train.
We go riding on a train.
That's how we get to school.

Walking Group: We go walking with our feet,
with our feet,
with our feet.
We go walking with our feet.
That's how we get to school.

All: No matter how we get to school,
get to school,
get to school.
No matter how we get to school.
We love to come to school!

The End

A Brand-New Year

Teacher: Welcome to _____
and the start
of a new school year.

All Children: We are in _____.
Let's give a cheer!

Teacher: Now I'd like to get to know you.
Can you tell me some of the things
that you would really like to do?

Child 1: Read books!

Child 2: Make friends!

Child 3: Draw pictures!

Child 4: Learn numbers!

Child 5: Have snacks!

Child 6: Hear stories!

Child 7: Do science!

• • • • • • ➤

Child 8:   Build with blocks!

Child 9:   Write poems!

Child 10:   Play games!

Child 11:   Sing songs!

Teacher: My, oh, my!
Our list is so long.
When should we start?

All Children: Right now!

The End

Many Ways to Say "Hello"

Group 1: In English, we say, "Hello!" (heh-LOW)

Group 2: In Japanese, we say, "Konnichiwa!" (koh-NEE-chee-wah)

Group 3: In Spanish, we say, "¡Hola!" (OH-lah)

Group 4: In Italian, we say, "Ciao!" (CHOW)

Group 5: In Hindi, we say, "Namasté!" (nah-mah-STAY)

........➤

Group 6: In Mandarin, we say,
"Ni hao!"
(nee HAOW)

Group 7: In Arabic, we say,
"Salaam!"
(sah-LAHM)

Group 8: In sign language, we say,

Group 9: In _____ , we say,

" _____ !"

All: Wow! Now we know
so many ways
to say, "Hello!"

The End

All About Us

Group 1: Our hair is brown
or blond or black
or any shade of red.

Group 2: It might be long
or short or straight
or curly on our heads.

Group 3: Our eyes are brown
or blue or green
or hazel, black, or gray.

Group 4: We're tall.
We're short.
We're in between.

All Groups: That's what our class
looks like today!

The End

Lost and Found

> **Characters**
> Children 1–13

Child 1:   Uh-oh.

Child 2:   What's wrong?

Child 1:   I lost my new hat!

Child 3:   We will help you look for it.

Child 4:   We will look around.

Child 5:   I will look in the classroom.

Child 6:   I will look in the Lost and Found.

Child 7:   I will look in the cubbies.
I will check them all.

Child 8:   I will look in the lunchroom.   • • • • • • ➤

Child 9: I will look in the hall.

Child 10: I will look in the bathroom.

Child 11: I will look in the gym.

Child 12: I will look on the playground.

Child 13: Did you ask the janitor, Tim?

Child 1: Uh-oh.

All Other Children: What's wrong?

Child 1: I found my hat!

All Other Children: Where was it?

Child 1: In my backpack!

The End

Fish School

Ms. Fish: Good morning, class!

All Student Fish: Good morning, Ms. Fish.

Ms. Fish: Today we will go over
our fish school rules.
What do we do if we
have something to say?

Student Fish 1:   We raise our fins!

Ms. Fish: Right. How do we sit
at our desks?

Student Fish 2:   With our tails on the floor.

Ms. Fish: Very good. What if you bring in a snack of worms?

Student Fish 3: Make sure you bring worms to share with everyone.

Ms. Fish: Yes. What if someone makes you mad?

Student Fish 4: Don't blow bubbles in someone's face! Try to talk it out.

Ms. Fish: Great work! Now, what would you like to learn about today?

All Student Fish: People!

The End

It's Cleanup Time!

Characters
Teacher
Children 1–8

Teacher: Children, it's cleanup time!

Child 1: It's cleanup time!
I will put away the blocks.

Child 2: It's cleanup time!
I can put them in this box.

Child 3: It's cleanup time!
I will pack up science kits.

Child 4: It's cleanup time!
I will pick up paper bits.

Child 5: It's cleanup time!
I will put away the books.

Child 6: It's cleanup time!
I will hang the smocks on hooks.

Child 7: It's cleanup time!
I will put the board games back.

Child 8: It's cleanup time!
I will pack the food from snack.

Teacher: Wow, you are all done!
Great job!
Now it's time for recess!
Now it's time for fun!

The End

Lunch Crunch

Characters
Children 1–7

Child 1:   When I eat lunch,
my crackers go crunch!

All: Crunchety, crunch, crunch!

Child 2:   When I eat lunch,
my carrots go crunch!

All: Crunchety, crunch, crunch!

Child 3:   When I eat lunch,
my pretzels go crunch!

All: Crunchety, crunch, crunch!

Child 4:   When I eat lunch,
my celery goes crunch!

All: Crunchety, crunch, crunch!

Child 5: When I eat lunch,
my apple goes crunch!

All: Crunchety, crunch, crunch!

Child 6: When I eat lunch,
my cookie goes crunch!

All: Crunchety, crunch, crunch!

Child 7: When we're done with lunch
our bags go crunch!

All: Crunchety, crunch, crunch!

The End

A Pie for Pigs

Characters

| Farmer | Pia Pig | Paco Pig |
| Polly Pig | Patty Pig | |

Farmer: Here, piggies.
Here, piggies.
Here is your snack.

Polly Pig: Oink, oink!
A pie for snack! Yummy!

Pia Pig: I like to eat pie!
That pie is all for me.

Patty Pig: Why is that pie just for you?

Pia Pig: Because . . .

Paco Pig: Because, why?

Pia Pig: Just because!

Polly Pig: But that is not fair.

Patty Pig: That pie is for
all of us to share.

Pia Pig: But I do not care!

Paco Pig: There is plenty of pie.

Polly Pig: We can each have a slice.

Pia Pig: Me, too?

**Polly, Patty,
and Paco Pig:**   Yes, of course!

Pia Pig: Okay, let's dig in!

All Pigs: Oink, Oink.
Mmmm-mmm.
We like pie!

The End

Good Manners

Sing to the tune of "Twinkle, Twinkle, Little Star"

Characters
Groups 1–9

Group 1: We say, "thank you."
We say, "please."

Group 2: We cover our noses
when we sneeze.

Group 3: We wash our hands
before having snack.

Group 4: We always put
the crayons back.

Group 5: We raise our hands
and don't call out.

Group 6: That way no one
has to shout.

• • • • • • ➤

Group 7:   To ask a question,
we wait our turn.

Group 8:   And in this way
we all can learn.

Group 9:   We say, "sorry,"
if we've been mean.

All: We work together.
We're a team!

The End

We Get Along

Child 1: May I build
blocks with you?

Child 2: I would like
it if you do.

Child 3: May I use
your crayons, please?

Child 4: I have extras.
You may use these.

Child 5: I would like
a drink of water, too.

Child 6: I will wait
and go after you.

Child 7: There is just one book.
We would you like to share?

Child 8: That is very kind.
You know how to be fair.

Child 9: After you read,
may I take a turn?

Child 10: Yes, you may.
So we both can learn.

Child 11: Are you hurt?
I saw you fall.

Child 12: Thank you for asking.
But I'm not hurt at all.

Child 13: Is there only
room for two?

Children 14–15: Sit down!
We'll make room for you.

........➤

Child 16:   Do you need help
tying your shoe?

Child 17:   Yes! It's nice to have
a friend like you!

Child 18:   May I borrow
that bottle of glue?

Child 19:   You can have this one.
It's brand new.

All: We like to share
to show we care.
We get along
the whole year long!

The End

With a Friend

Characters
Children 1–11

Child 1:   You can talk with a friend.

Child 2:   You can walk with a friend

Child 3:   and make a friend who is new.

Child 4:   You can play with a friend.

Child 5:   You can stay with a friend

Child 6:   and learn about fun things to do.

Child 7:   You can eat with a friend.

Child 8:   You can meet with a friend

Child 9:   and sometimes even get mad.

Child 10:   You can ride with a friend.

Child 11:   You can hide with a friend.

All: Having friends makes us all glad!

The End

New in School

Characters
Dan
Min

Dan: Hi, my name is Dan.
What is your name?

Min: My name is Min.

Dan: Are you new here?

Min: Yes, I am.

Dan: Do you like this school?

Min: It is all so new to me.
I do not know yet.

Dan: I like to read.
Do you like to read?

Min: Yes, I like to read.

Dan: I like to paint.
Do you like to paint?

Min: Yes, I like to paint.

Dan: I like to hop.
Do you like to hop?

Min: Yes, I like to hop.

Dan: Show me how you hop.

Min: Hop! Hop! Hop!

Dan: You are a good hopper!

Min: Thank you.

Dan: Would you like to be friends?

Min: Yes, I would like that.

Dan: Let's go hopping.

Both: Hop! Hop! Hop!

The End

Reading Friends

Suki: Would you like to read with me?
I have a new book.

Alex: Sure! Let me take a look.

Suki: How about if
we read over there?

Alex: We can both fit
on this rocking chair.

Suki: It's big enough
for us both to share.

Alex: I will read one page.

Suki: I will read the next.

Alex: We can take turns.

Suki: Once upon a time,
there were three bears,

Alex: a father bear,

Suki: a mother bear,

Alex: and a baby bear.

Suki: One day. . .

Alex: What do you think
will happen next?

Suki: I don't know
but let's try to guess!

Teacher: Class! It's time for lunch.

Alex: I did not know
it was so late!

Suki: To read the rest,
we will have to wait.

Alex: After we eat,
do you want to meet?

Suki: Sure! We can come back
to this same seat!

Alex: Okay, see you later.
It's a date.

Suki: See you later!
I can't wait!

The End

We Like to Cook!

Teacher: Who wants to make
applesauce today?

Whole Class: We do! We do!
Hurray! Hurray!

Teacher: Where do we start?
What do we need?
Here are the steps.
Who wants to read?

Child 1: First:
Chop up the apples.

Child 2: Second:
Put them in a pot.

Child 3: Third:
Add water, sugar,
and spice—just a spot.

· · · · · · · ▶

Child 4: Fourth:
Put the pot on the stove.
Then cook and stir a lot.

Child 5: Fifth:
Cook until the apples
get soft and very hot.

Child 6: Mmmm! It smells so good.
I can't wait until it's done!

Teacher: The applesauce is ready.
Who would like to have some?

Whole Class: We do! We do!
Applesauce for everyone!
Making applesauce
is so much fun!

The End

Show and Tell

Characters
Mark   Kia
1st-Grade Class   2nd-Grade Class

Mark: For show and tell
I brought my 5 pet worms.
1-2-3-4-5.
In this cup are Slim, Swim, Jim, Tim, and Kim.

1st-Grade Class: Wow! Worms!

Kia: I brought my 5 pet snakes.
1-2-3-4-5.
In this cage are Slinky, Dinky,
Pinky, Stinky, and . . .
Oh, no! Where's Binky?
Binky got out!

1st-Grade Class: E-e-e-e-k! SNAKES!

Kia: Is Binky under a desk?
He likes to crawl.

1st-Grade Class: E-e-e-e-k!

Kia: Is Binky under the sink?
He likes water to drink.

**1st-Grade
Class:** E-e-e-e-k!

Kia: Is Binky in a cubby?
He likes to look for
things to eat.

**2nd-Grade
Class:** E-e-e-e-k!

Mark: Why is the class next door
yelling?

Kia: They found Binky!

The End

Mary Went to the Library

Sing to the tune of "Mary had a Little Lamb"

> **Characters**
> Groups 1–4

Group 1: Mary wanted a book to read, book to read, book to read.

Group 2: Mary wanted a book to read. So she went to the library.

Group 3: She found many books to read, books to read, books to read.

Group 4: She found many books to read and checked one out for home.

Group 1: She sat down and read all day, read all day, read all day.

Group 2: She sat down and read all day. She read the book at home.

Group 3: Soon it was time to return the book, return the book, return the book.

Group 4: It was time to return the book, back to the library.

All: Now Mary goes there every week, every week, every week. Now Mary goes there every week for a library book to read!

The End

Let's Play!

Characters
Children 1–8

Child 1: Jump!

Child 2: Run!

Child 3: Hop!

Child 4: Skip!

Child 5: Twirl!

Child 6: Swing!

Child 7: Climb!

Child 8: Slide!

All: These are some of the things
we like to do outside!

The End